Bukowski in Love
by MC Lars

Bukowski in Love

**Copyright © 2007 MC Lars. All rights reserved.
Printed in the United States of America.**

**For more information, write Horris Press,
345 7th Ave., 24th FL, New York NY 10001**

FIRST EDITION

www.mclars.com

for Jay

"Who need be afraid of the merge?"
- Walt Whitman

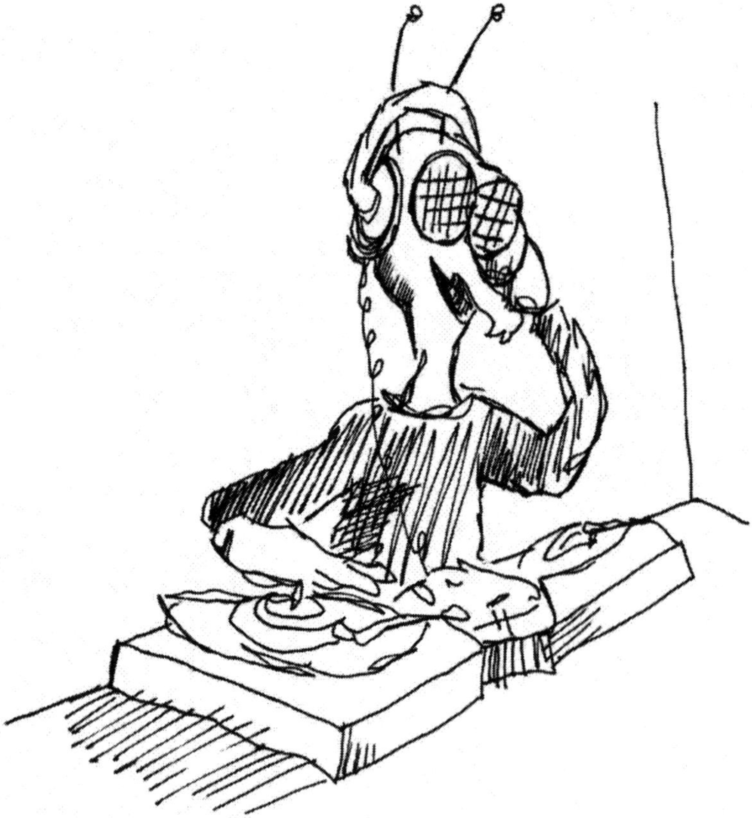

Contents

Intro

Jesus Don't Want Me for a Faucet	1
Taco Bell	2
Charles Schulz and the Immortality Blanket	5
They Cut My Spaceship Chord because they Disliked Me	6
Desensitized	9
My Music Career	10
The Knife	13
Ducks	14
Amtrak and Happy Endings	17
Fishing for Piranhas	18
Water as a Metaphor for Something Important	21
On Leaving Your House in Carmel to Go on Tour	22
My Fear Bat	25
On Saying Goodbye to My Best Friend Before Going off to College	26
Testimony	29
Pimples	30
The Trouble with Ghosts	33
Kissing You Is Like Sticking My Tongue in the Light Socket	34
Wilson Fields	37
Reinventing John S. Hall	38
Upon First Hearing Marilyn Manson	41
Law School is for Pussies	42
On Intellectual Property	45
Girlfriends Are Overrated	46
To the Rude Driver	49
Carmel Valley	50
I Wrote This in the Computer Lab at Stanford University	53
Dodge to Freedom	54
Grandpa Bob	57
Drown Me in the Sea	58
Reciprocated Soliloquy	61
Siena	62
Resonant Hearts, Co-Ops	65
August	66
Gatorade	69
Kerouac : His Muse :: Me : You	70
Bukowski in Love	73
nerves	74
I Am an Alien	77
Confirmation Day	78
The Hot Girl Who Works at This Summer Camp with Me Should Visit My Bunk More Often	81
October 31st, 1998	82
Stoned in Denver	85
Shelf Life	86

The first gangsta rap record was more brutal than anything you could possibly imagine. It was the story of a hardcore player who was so vicious that if you dissed him, he would rip off your arms and decapitate your mom.

If anyone tried to mess with this gangsta's posse, he would take them out with his gigantic weapon of choice. He was truly ruthless, and like any true player, when he died he was buried with his pimp cup.

I know what you're thinking. I must be talking about Tupac Shakur or Eazy E right? No. Gangsta rap has a long history, going back at least thirteen hundred years.

Check out the 8th century heroic epic poem *Beowulf*, which had all of the elements of a 50 Cent album — violence, slang, intricate rhymes, specific repeating rhythms, and a hero fighting against all odds.

Hip-hop is a postmodern continuation of this oral tradition. Rappers tell stories to pass on culture and information in an easy to remember way. As KRS-One said in 1987, "Poetry is the language of imagination, poetry is a form of positive creation" ("Poetry" from *Criminal Minded*). And that sums it up.

I could go on and on about the correlations between old-school literature and hip-hop culture, but I'll save that for later. Come talk to me about it at a show, I'm a nerd and we can break it down until the bouncers tell us they are closing the club and try to kick us out. Then we can talk about it in the parking lot.

In the meantime, here's a book of various poems I've written over the past ten years. I did the drawings with Rapidograph pens and scanned them so the pages would be more interesting.

Keep it fresh.

MC LARS
Lancaster, PA
October 4th, 2007

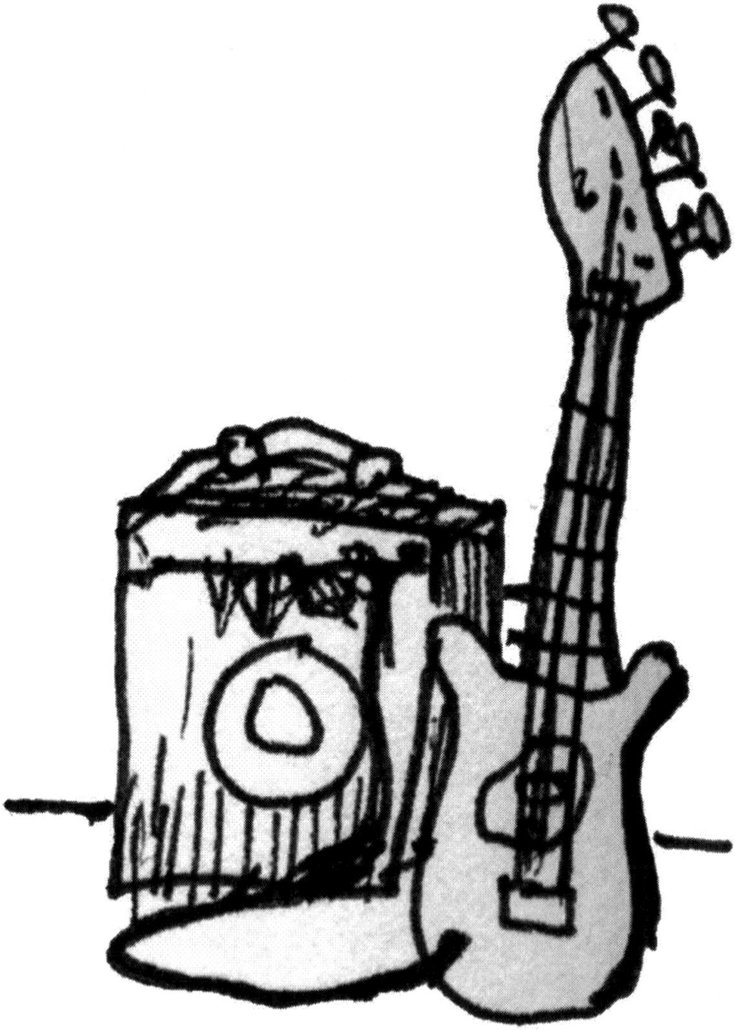

Jesus Don't Want Me for a Faucet

Hey Kurt Cobain the pain of lyricism
is nothing to scoff at when it scathes
slaved over so it's heard for a moment
your Pacific Northwest pain alive there
your responsibility today there —
                    generation X spokesman.

I value your left hand creativity Kurt -
metallic motion magnetic synthesis
generator principle amplified.
Alienated wails of bipolar
brain chemistry, commerce, media
icon formation.

That's the beauty of the punk rock faucet, though.
Turn it on and let the spirit soar!
Like the young Homer Jay Simpson -
Ugly and real.

Too much to handle sometimes?
"Let's plug up the hole," you said
Leaking too much truth it was uneven,

Teenage spirit effervescent Kurt
Adrift in the sea,
finally free, now walking on it.

August, 2002

Taco Bell

The Taco Bell lady is mad at me
I let people in after she closed down shop
but there's no need to fight
cholesterol tastes like chicken
and the line of customers
wraps around the block!

April, 2007

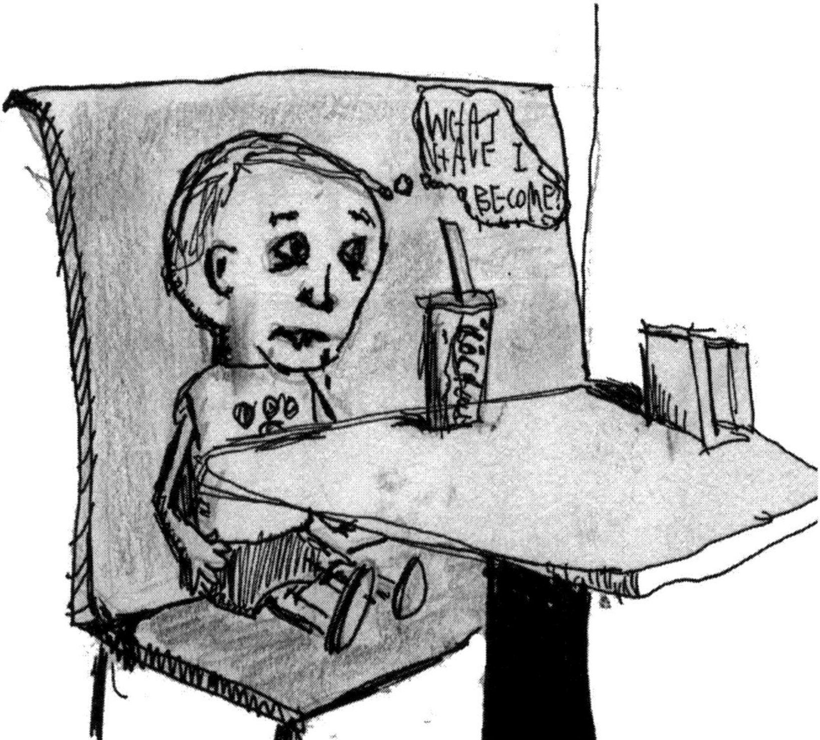
WHAT HAVE I BE-COME?

4

Charles Schulz and the Immortality Blanket

So, Lucy my dear, I'm not sorry
It will never be my time —
You may pull that football away forever
But I will continue on
until the end,
with my zigzag shirt
and bald head
full of truth
and optimistic epiphanies.

You can't kill me
because even after I die
I'm still here.

You can't kill me,
I'm perpetually petulant!
I will stay in the crevices forever,
in the minds of people I know
in their ears as songs
on the hard drives of immortality,
.mp3's and .jpg's,
yeah I'm here and always will be.

And when I watch news reels that say
maybe there's no reason for anything
I laugh and change the channel.
My Hannity & Colmes analysis is more
Buddha than Bukowski.

Just like Linus
with his blanket on lock-down
well aware of the rules we chose to play by.

Charles Schulz once told me
that his greatest fear was dying,
lying seventy-two inches deep
not having made a difference.

"You've already made a difference to me,
see," I said. "You gave me life."

August, 2002

They Cut My Spaceship Chord Because They Disliked Me

August 1st, 1987
floating
floating
floating
it's been four hours almost!

just because i ate all of the astronaut ice cream,
just because i would wake
    up the crew in the middle of the night
    to tell them that we were being eaten by aliens:

    my "comrades" had to get even.

sending me out to readjust the tail fins
and then slamming the door,
they snipped my cord.

    okay guys, it's not funny anymore
    seriously, it's not funny anymore.

September, 1999

CALL WAITING.

8

Desensitized

      i am sixteen and sitting in the
      theater with my favorite Primus shirt.

"Poor little baby deer,"
      exclaims the child behind me.

      because just then in the movie
      a little baby deer
      was shot by
      a thoughtless
      human predator.

      and i
      know why
      no one else
      in the theater
      exclaims empathy
      for the baby dear also :

           too many senseless deaths
               to have to cry for one more.

"Poor little baby deer,"
      the child behind me exclaims,
      yet I ask myself:

           Who do I really feel sorry for?

December, 1998

My Music Career

I used to sit in my bedroom
and write songs for my friends to listen to.
Now I sit in my bedroom
and write songs for my friends to listen to.
Fourteen years old forever, baby!!!

October, 2007

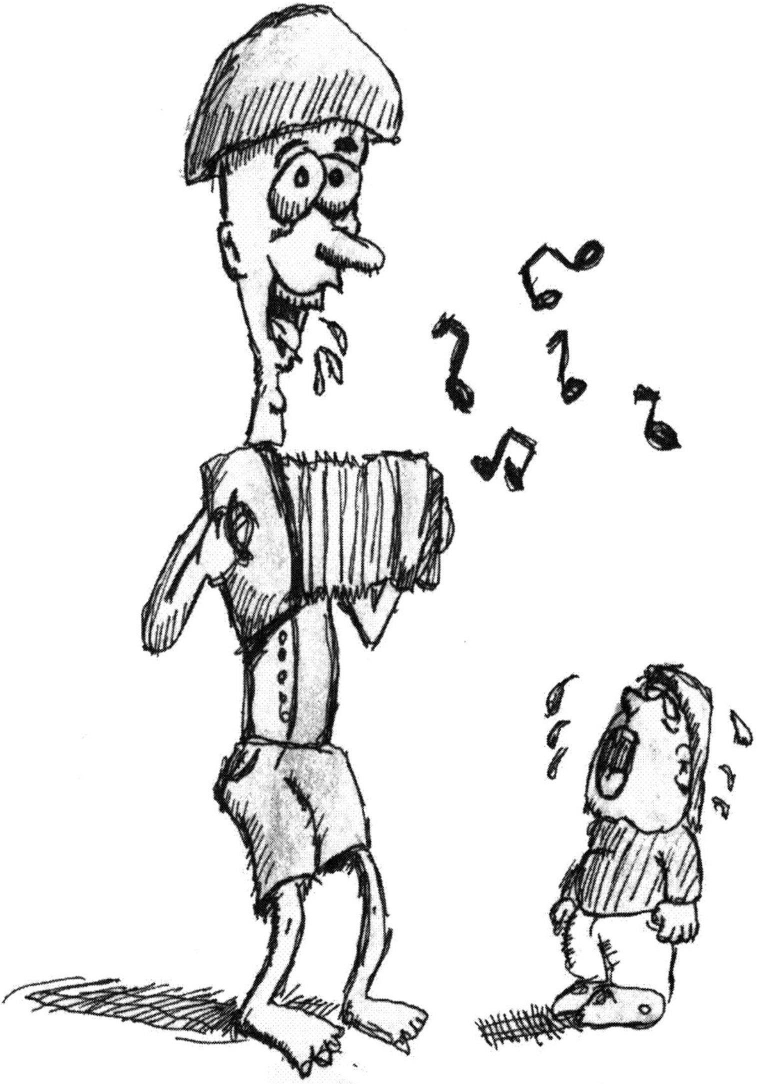

12

The Knife

The Knife I once used to
    m   ut i la   t e
insects (a few years back) in my sad
sadomasochistic   formative years

I am now using to cut a picture
I drew of you
    out of this well worn collection
of drawings that I'm holding!

    Sometimes it's funny, how the pain
    you administrate
    eventually comes back at you
        tenfold

February, 1999

Ducks

They talk like lost priests,
Walk like lonely nurses,
And dream like over-paid lawyers.

May, 2000

15

BUCK

16

Amtrak and Happy Endings

lying here inside your tent
the crickets chirp outside
the air is clean, your body's soft
your lips are so smooth

I had a dream that night
lying naked next to you
that I was a DJ
and everything I played was the best song ever

the needle dropped
the records spun
no need to ask
what to play next

I want to make you happy
like you've made me
on this sleepy morning

funny how right it feels
getting lost in your eyes
with no Amtrak schedule:

sharing silly stories
she's so sexy and smart
soft and delicate
strong-willed and serious
too beautiful for words

and it's scary, Ana,

because sometimes
this shit
just happens …

August, 2007

Fishing for Piranhas

I'm circling this lake in my boat
As eager piranhas hop aboard,
arrogant, digesting,
peeling away my fat,
crawling into my head
laughing at me.

They hop into my boat:
"Feed me, feed me, feed me, me, me!"

The irony is funny at first and then:
No longer, I say
please
please stop pulling!

But
they jump in, thousands,
they flop and make plans,
conniving, biting,
grinning,
in a demonic death march
of teeth on skin,
my blood reflecting
    the morning sun.

The boat flips,
My bones sink.

August, 2002

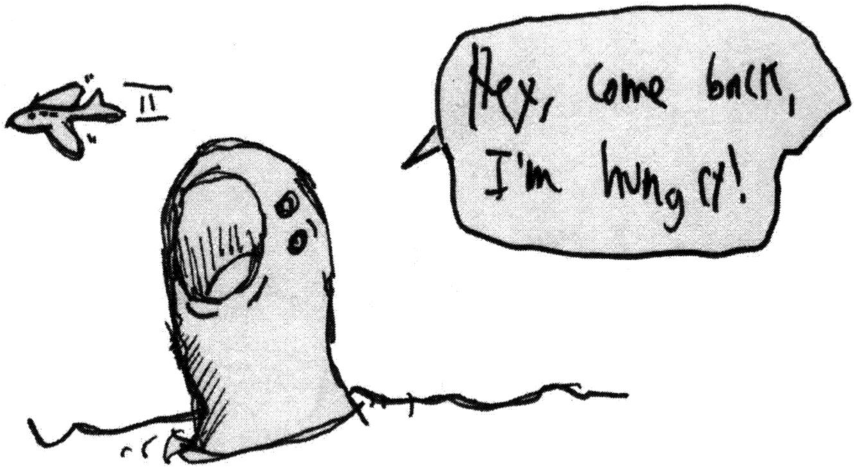
Hey, come back,
I'm hungry!

20

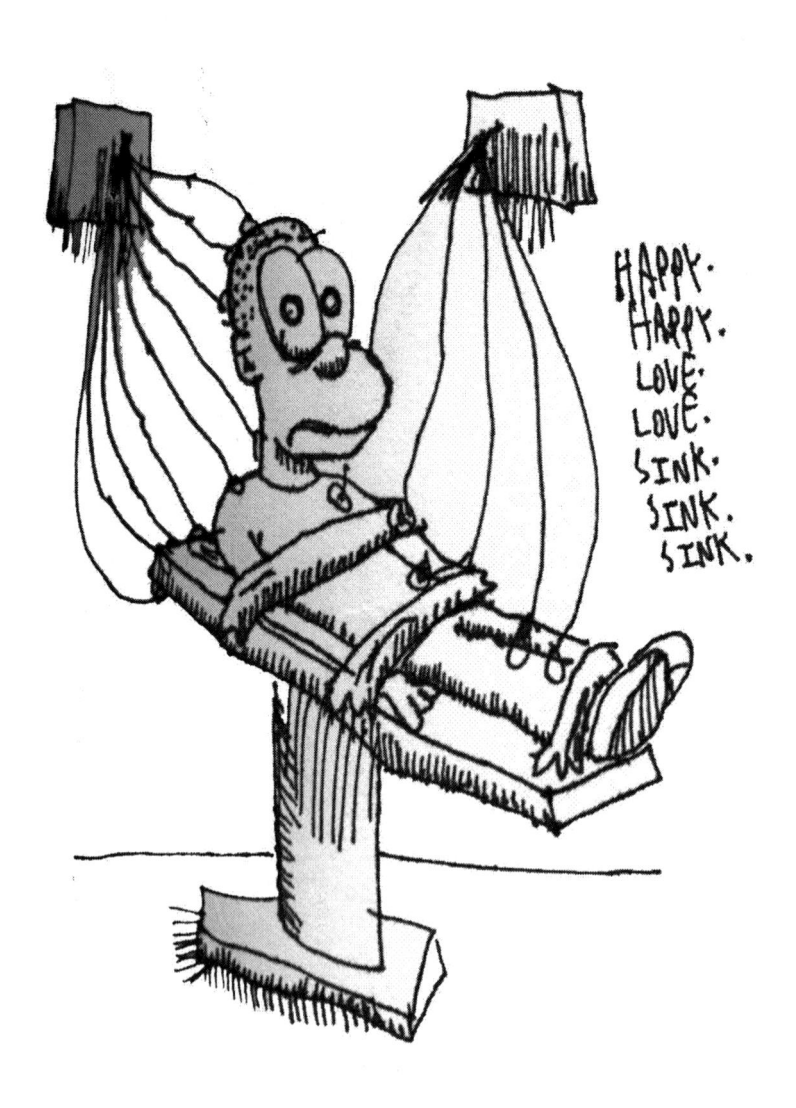

Water as a Metaphor for Something Important

Ice can kill you fill you up
Give me that frozen throne when I'm fifty
When I can't get it up it will be hilarious!

Funny is falling down the stairs
Funny is falling off of a cliff
Funny is falling from a building
And then lying there
Until they move you off of the ice, see
It's cold when rains.

That's objectivity -
No one cares if someone
Left the Guernica out in the storm because
Rain solidifies and rain delivers
Sheets at your feet
We can't help but stand on them reluctantly.

August, 2002

On Leaving Your House in Carmel to Go on Tour

Sometimes I puke all over my self
in diabolical rage

cigarettes in my arm
I am so drunk tonight
I hate myself for drinking
dizzy spindles of narcissism
and warm shits in the toilet
make me think of the Phish concert

decorating the tree
I caught that fleeting moment in the back of my mind
you and me and the tree and my parents
and those December nights

Discovery!

I go insane sometimes

I'm on the road in a flurry
With no home base
And a stack of DVD's.

November, 2004

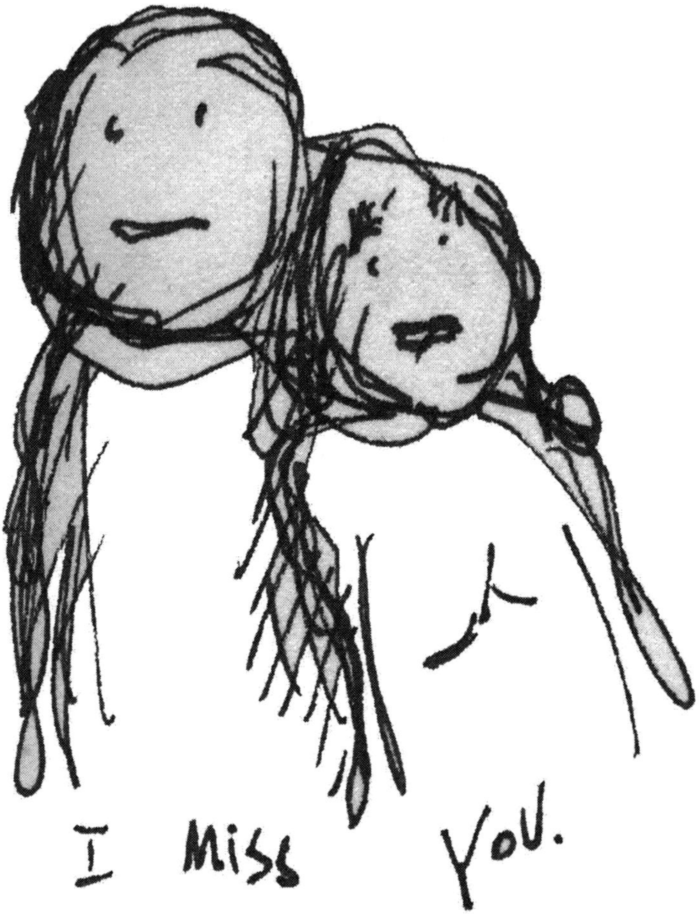
I MISS YOU.

24

My Fear Bat

Fear can sit on your face at night
Laughing as you gasp for air
Fear can bite you in the ass while you sleep
Laughing as you try to smack it away
Fear can take the air out of your tires
Fear can close your finger in the window of your car
Fear can rip the soles of your shoes off
      Like super strength adhesive from hell

But when I've got my fear bat
I smack fear in the face
And tell it to stop being such a little bitch

On Saying Goodbye to My Best Friend Before Going Off to College

Chris
high school was awesome thanks to you
who knew this roly-poly P.G. fun-boy
would be that high school friend
                    'till the end.

Chris I want to be like Wesley Willis
and name my album after you
"You are my friend to the end.
You are my friend forever more,
in Jesus."
Yeah.

Chris let's break down the life events
In my skull courtesy of you:

> Goober peas, Tahoe, Ho-Yon,
> Elendor, the Blues Brothers, old Mary Poppins men,
> Gilbert and/or Sullivan, N64, the Who,
> Pink Floyd, Jethro Tull, Washington D.C.,
> East Coast college tours, getting lost in Boston,
> movies, scripts, KSPB and that's just the start.

Chris we're in touch off and on
though New York likes you
I like you too. So
please stay bouncy in my soul
you are a beautiful freak of
nature like me
I'll miss you but we'll meet again.

                sincerely andrew

August, 2001

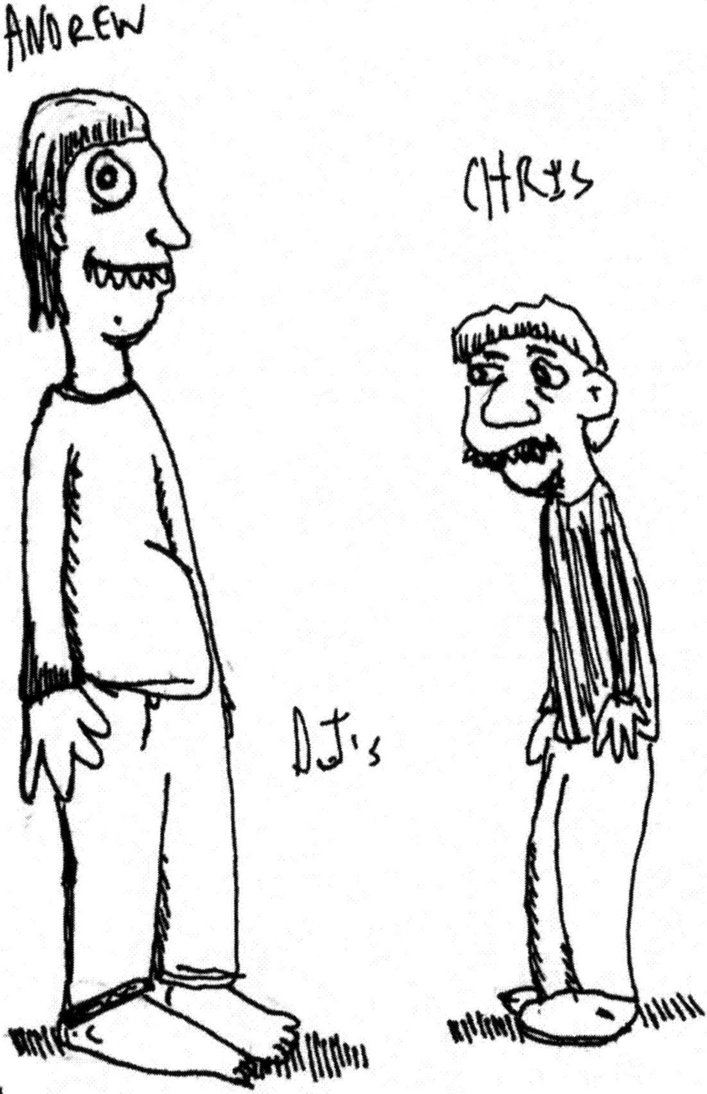

MORNING MADNESS; FRIDAYS 6-8 ON
KSPB 91.9 FM

DR. JONES IS CURED

Testimony

"I think you're funnier when you're
off your medication," she once told me.
"You're more entertaining."

"Okay then," I responded.
"So from now on, dear, no more Prozac."

Honestly, judge,
and for these reasons,
I am not responsible for the
sudden and
savage murder of my wife.

November, 1999

Pimples

They always come in groups:
odd, un-symmetrical,
unchoreographed gibberish.

On the lower left corner of my chin,
behind my ears, between my eyes,
those deformed triangular blemishes.

And I hate it when my pimples
resemble constellations,
concentrated in league
on the bacteria-infested areas
of my adolescent epidermis.

"Get yourself some Clearasil,"
someone once told me,
yet my situation is genetic:
I can not help being
the poster boy for brand-x.
You see I'm pizza face,
with extra toppings.

I only wish you would look
beyond my pimples,
and kiss me for who I am inside.

April, 2000

31

The Trouble with Ghosts

The trouble with ghosts
is that they forget
when to say goodbye.

Case in point:
this ghost comes again
every night
making me chilly
and flickering the lights
in my Carmel Valley room.

And I say, "you there, stop!"
but it's not a solution.

Ghosts are like reluctant college kids
who never quite felt comfortable
in high school assembly
but keep coming back
for second period.

July, 2002

Kissing You Is Like Sticking My Tongue in the Light Socket

And I fell down again
and I'm not sure when I'm near or far
my tongue is shocked
you're so ridiculously fine
I want you and it's insane

That's not the way it works, we know
that's not the way it works, you show
youth is fast old age is slow!

But you're so freaking beautiful
it's kind of ridiculous

And as you leave the room
my lower stomach hurts so warm,
I'm falling into Highway One traffic
as cars skid everywhere in a chaotic ballet

I hate solitude at times like this
memories of abandonment
with no connection to the broader world,
a remote control in my right hand,
an empty tube of KY jelly,
resting in the fetal position
on your gray IKEA table.

December, 2004

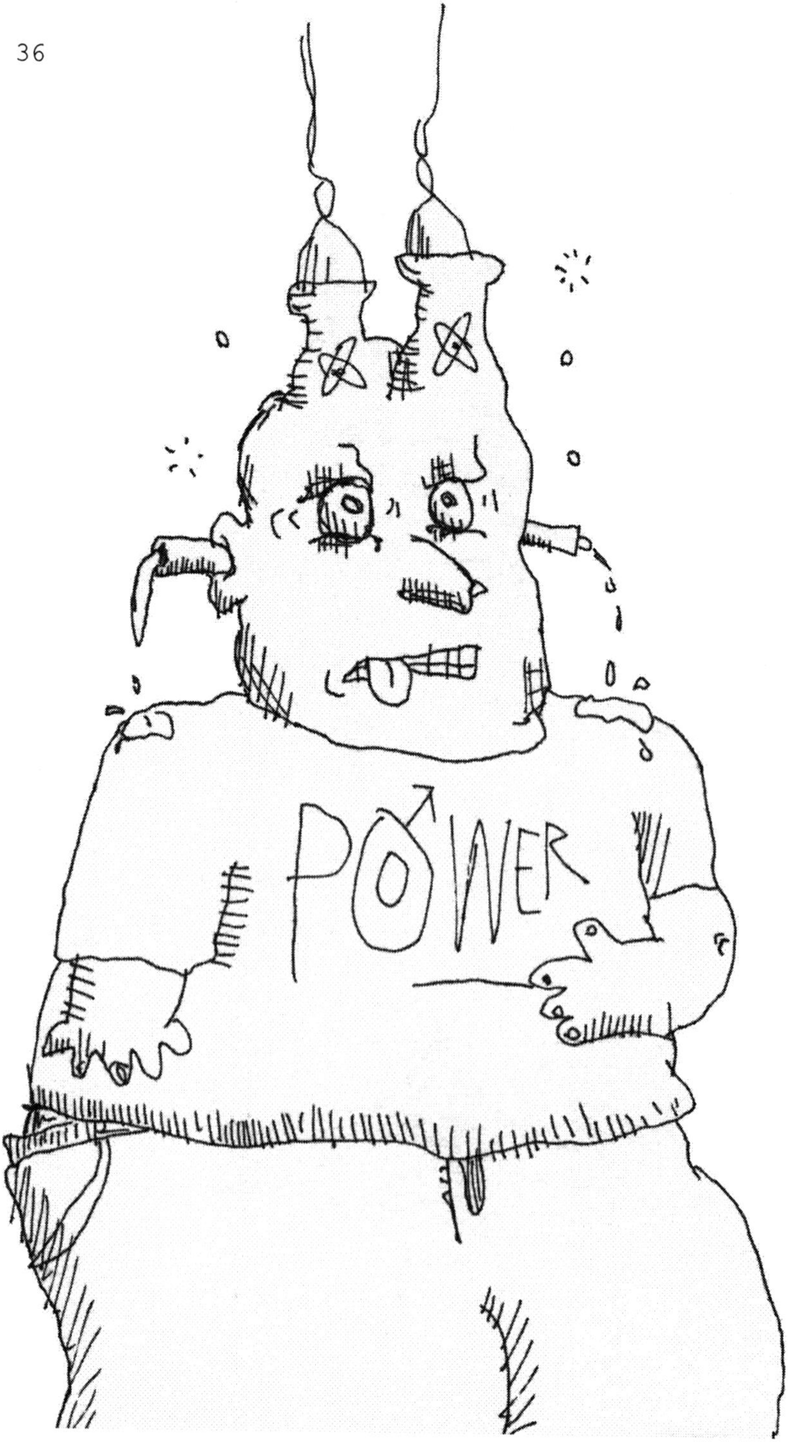
POWER

Wilson Fields

In Wilson Fields
The mushrooms grow.
Not side by side,
But in a row.

On seeing them,
I thought it neat,
If I took
One or two to eat --

Like, Mario, then
I might jump...

    But now I need
    My stomach pumped.

December, 1999

Reinventing John S. Hall

Tonight I sit
Somewhere between gravity and weightlessness
Telling stories into a broken microphone
As the major labels get impatient,
My legacy: a hidden feature on the Beavis & Butt-head DVD

Spitting on a blank page
To put out the incessant fire

Falling somewhere deep between
The bowels of popular culture
And Bukowski's breakdown

Disinterested in anything
Indie roots getting so weak
They coerce themselves to let go

I want to vomit
Purge the sickness of rock star dreams
That sometimes die too soon!

Sitting between the paper and the stars
A pen in my urethra
Screaming quietly.

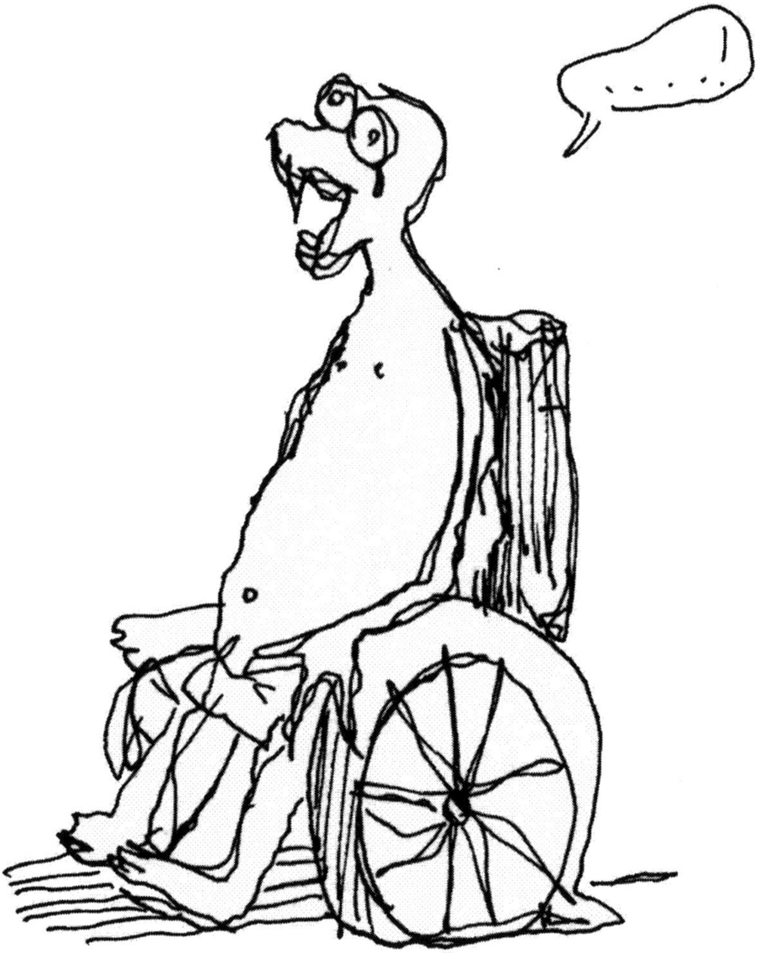

40

Upon First Hearing Marilyn Manson

```
    Four
         No
            Five
     Stars     in      the  dark
                dark
navy             blue
        sky
  caught      my      eye
         with     a
large      hook      from           some story
            of  some      fractured
         warrior
               yearning
    for    light
  apart
                              from
          the              night.
```

        (when self-induced alienation
        can be beautiful too.)

Law School is for Pussies

Every day growing up
I see people in normal situations.
I want to be normal.
I want to be able to go up to a bar,
meet a cool girl,
converse with her about something normal,
and then take her home.

None of this desperate-comedian-gone-lost
-on-the-world-broken-hearted-beat-synced-poet-bullshit!

Because hey!!
Wouldn't that be amazing?

To pass the bar exam
And move to the suburbs?
Safety in isolation.
I could hide behind a quirky,
nervous façade,
my six figure salary
and Martha Stewart paint jobs
getting brittle and pathetic with age.

Couldn't I just have a suit
and nice hair
and leather shoes
and a sense of belonging
and leave the tree fort in the yard?

When the crayons start to melt
selling out smells so sweet
to those with car payments
and little to say.

WHEN I WAS FOUR I WANTED TO BE AN ASTRONAUT. BUT THEN I GREW UP AND BECAME A BUISNESS MAN. I WANT TO KILL MYSELF NOW.
MAYBE I SHOULD HAVE STUCK WITH MY INITIAL IMPULSES?

Rock & Roll Pussy

On Intellectual Property

I stole four chords today
From a song I figured out.
So who can say that they weren't earned?
No one, without a doubt -

Yet I guess it won't be long
Untill you're all alone,
Reading from a well known book
To see I also stole this poem!

April, 1999

Girlfriends Are Overrated

Let go the dog won't leave
and if he does you're better off solo.
So low pulling me into the dirt
bamboo in my skin like Australia
ingrained Koala toy and girlfriends to hold me
when grandparents die? Independence

    See I'm fine and

I'll just let go see
if the dog comes back
to me (trite) it was meant to be.

    i.e. this is a metaphor:
    now for females no more leashes
    I unleash friendship
    but not my soul it's mine
    ladies:

        "My music comes first
        you'll never be number one."

    Take a second to swim laps
    Rolling Stone, Alfred E. Neuman, and AOL

Well I'm happy now ladies
let's just walk.

August, 2002

47

48

To the Rude Driver

So how do you spell asshole?
KP3F42
(that was his license plate)

Carmel Valley

Suburban on Highway One, left on G16,
Carmel Valley road.

To offer us what?
I've felt derailed ever since
we left Oakland,
I'm 19 now.
Last year we drove past you,
The first Monterey house,
5 Victoria Vale,
my ex-girlfriend and me,
you were done up in pine needles.
I've stopped playing with Ninja Turtles.
Time won't stop, even for the Technodrome.

We kissed under the Carmel Valley moon once,
after the jazz festival
but forgot the anniversary.
"Too cold" Sarah said.

Sarah you once drew our view from the window
with colored pencils
alive and ardent
the sun engulfing -
Sarah I wish I hadn't torn it up.

But I was ready to go.
"All my bags were packed."

I found something in Carmel Valley
standing on that turn:
Garland Ranch, the Grade, the Village,
the warm smell of Oak,
Joy by my side,
"Good girl."

When the sun hits
Milton's Eden,
you couldn't stay even if you wanted to.
The apple supply is limited
and rarely are they free.

August, 2002

SICK PAIN I HATE LONELINESS

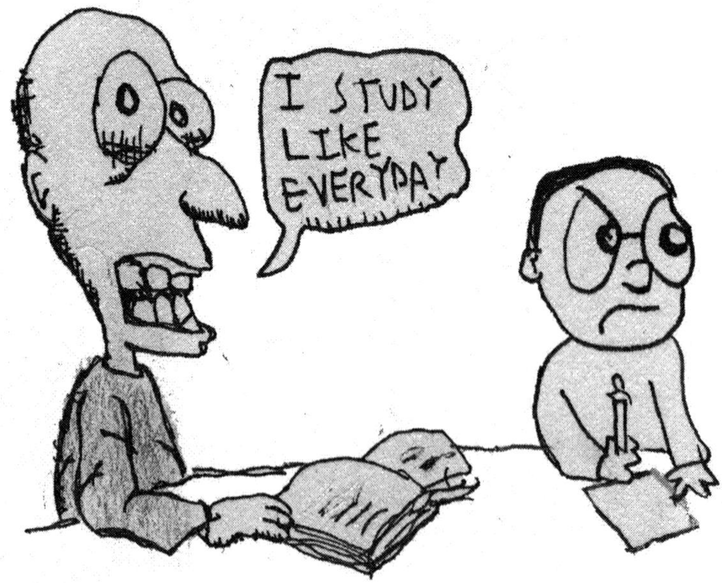
I STUDY LIKE EVERYDAY

I Wrote This In the Computer Lab at Stanford University

I dislike:
fat people who smoke and cuss,
trash left in once-pristine locations,
ardent proponents of TRL,
violent teenagers with ill-informed opinions,
white people in SUVs,
your t-shirt that says "Princess" in sparkling letters,
spoiled children who bite their parents,
your loquacious wife with nothing to say,
and
    the antisocial drones with no sense of humor
    at this missile building university.

June, 2002

Dodge to Freedom

Get in your 1989 Dodge and go
drive all over the country
like Jack Kerouac back on track
but don't stop for Wendy's,
Taco Bell, In-n-Out Burger or hitchhikers
just accelerate away
otherwise you may forget.

Leave your wife and two daughters -
Claire, 6, with the bottle cap glasses and
Anna, 1,
who cries and kicks at the beach
wrapped in the angry towel because
you spoiled her-
her temper tantrum flaring like a book of matches
you pull her close to comfort her
but your little bitch of a daughter bites you hard
above your right nipple,
you scream
and place Anna down
you should have thrown her down
on her face, homie.

Yeah, get in that Dodge
you can't afford a relationship
with anyone but yourself and
the walls smell bad again
(like soft cheese and paint),
your pets can feed themselves and
your wife just bought new batteries
for her vibrator.   (Bzzzzzzzzzz)
Yes, your children might trip and bite
and sweat and scream.
But they will find themselves.

It's up to you to roll,
unlock the domestic shackles for a minute,
suburbia will always be there waiting.

July, 2002

55

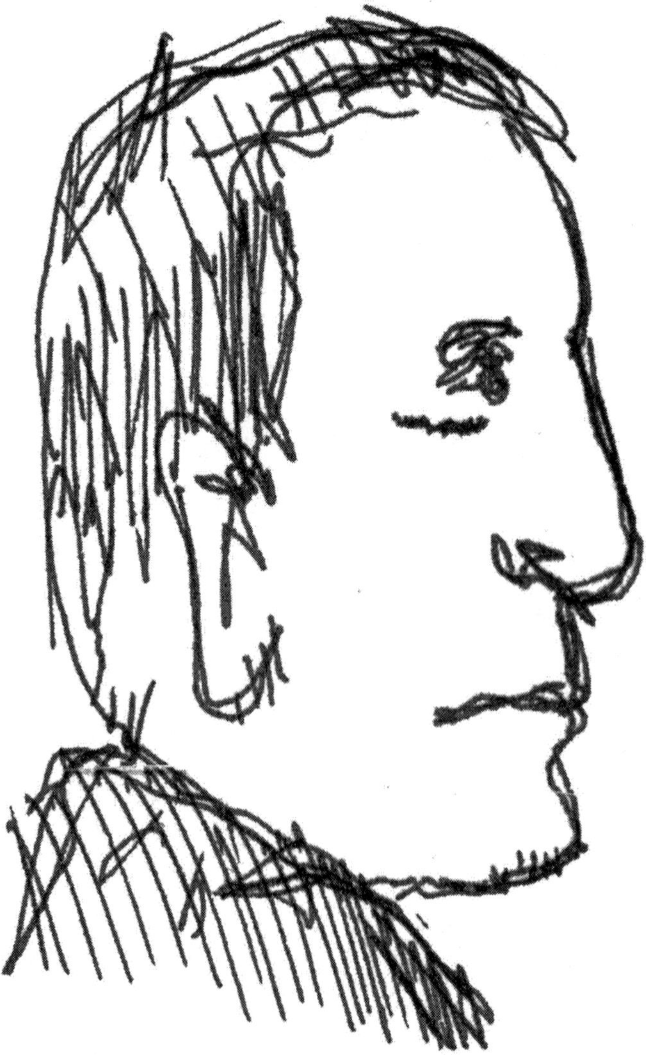

Grandpa Bob

You died the summer before I started college.
The same Grandpa who had sent me a postcard everyday
when I went off to summer camp.

And now I miss our trips to Sacramento
your Airedale Laddie
your old couches
microwaved dinners
with mom, dad, Sarah, you and Nana.

Forgotten ties
A.A. Meetings
Questions unanswered

I always thought you would be here forever.
We could talk about WWII some more
Your flights over Germany
The bombs and the victory
The history and the legend
The story you loved to tell.

These days my world expands
And everything they've taught me crumbles.

After you died,
We cleaned out your house and I found your journals:
on the entry for the day I was born
you wrote how pleased you were
how excited
how real.

I never knew how you felt that day.

But you knew I loved you,
And maybe somehow through the stories
you'd be forgiven.

It's those little things that count,
They mean everything,
in the end.

October, 2002

Drown Me in the Sea

Drown me in the sea
and let my bloated corpse wash up onto shore.
Then kick me in the face,
as my over-hydrated spine snaps in half
under the force of your angry shoe.
Then eat my organs.

(but please, without cheese)

July, 2000

59

60

Reciprocated Soliloquy

Well sometimes Hamlet and I
Have Danishes and tea
We talk about lonely angels
And how one can become free.

To be or not to be?
I guess that is the question,
As we sit in contemplation
Or casual reflection.

But sometimes the Prince and I
Go running late at night
And when the full moon leads the way
I know that everything's all right.

Because nature's often beautiful
And life, it can be dear
And when I talk to Hamlet,
He tries to make this clear.

June, 2000

`Siena`

down the hill together with the group
she's right in front of me (i used to love her)
sweat and sunshine as we plow and peddle
up and down the undulating Italian countryside
the heat overcomes, then is followed
by refreshing june rain
(baptized in another country)

her bike stops, the chain sticks
and i stop to help her -
she wants to know how i know so much about bikes,
i ride them often i say - she smiles

i fix the finicky chain and we
ride back towards the hotel

       (yet the further along we go,
        i know, the further apart we grow)

`June, 2000`

Siena
6-29-00

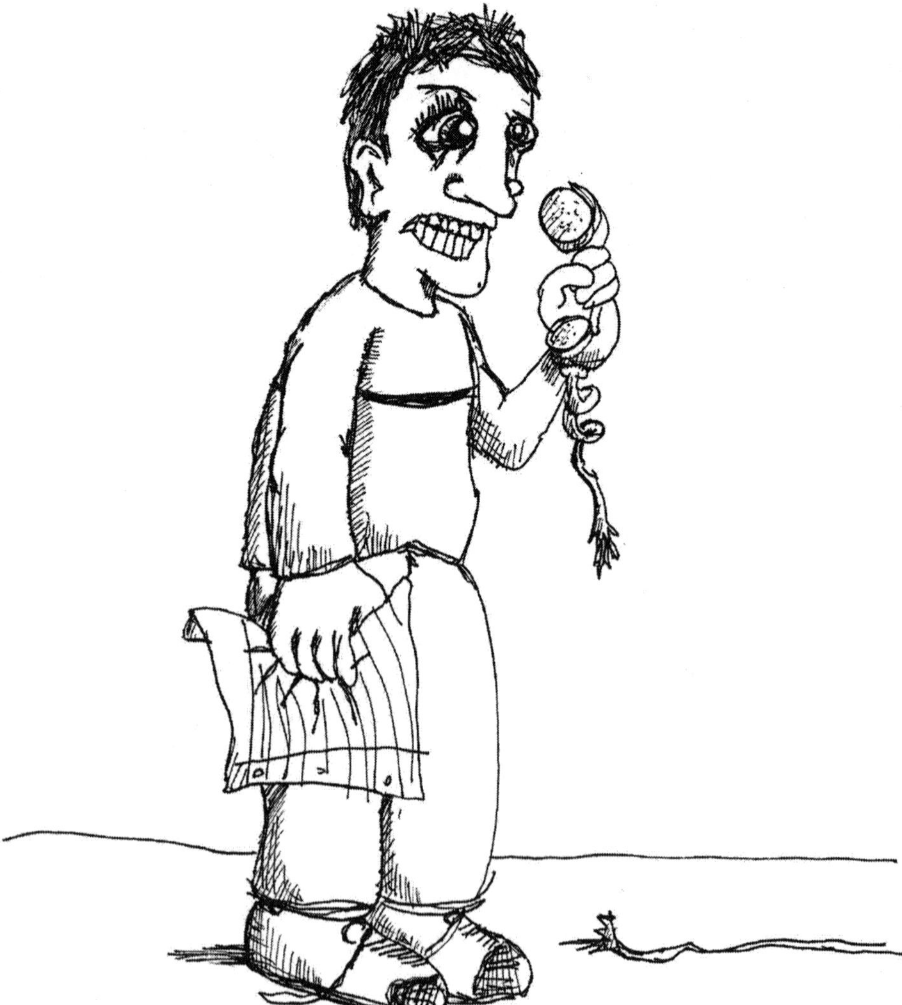

Resonant Hearts, Co-Ops

Last night the moonlight
reflected on your face at the
Mayfield co-op (Friday, room 211).

My lips against your cheek,
against your hand, against my soul.

As free as Holden Caulfield and Sally Hayes,
no apprehension,
holding on for a few more minutes.

Did you notice how I'm wired?
Sad, rusty, built last-minute.
Pushing off your questions,
with dissonant silence.

An awkward knee-jerk reaction.
All I'm saying is
I want to skip my classes
and take fifteen units of you.

I want to burn any books that bring me down.
That's how you make me feel.
Cautiously ignorant.

Pure bliss.

See, my world is humming now
like a cell phone on vibrate:

(beep)   "1 new message"

Since when did my heart
get this many bars?

September, 2002

August

A great time to
burn your television.

PASS ON CULTURE WITH MUCH PATIENCE.

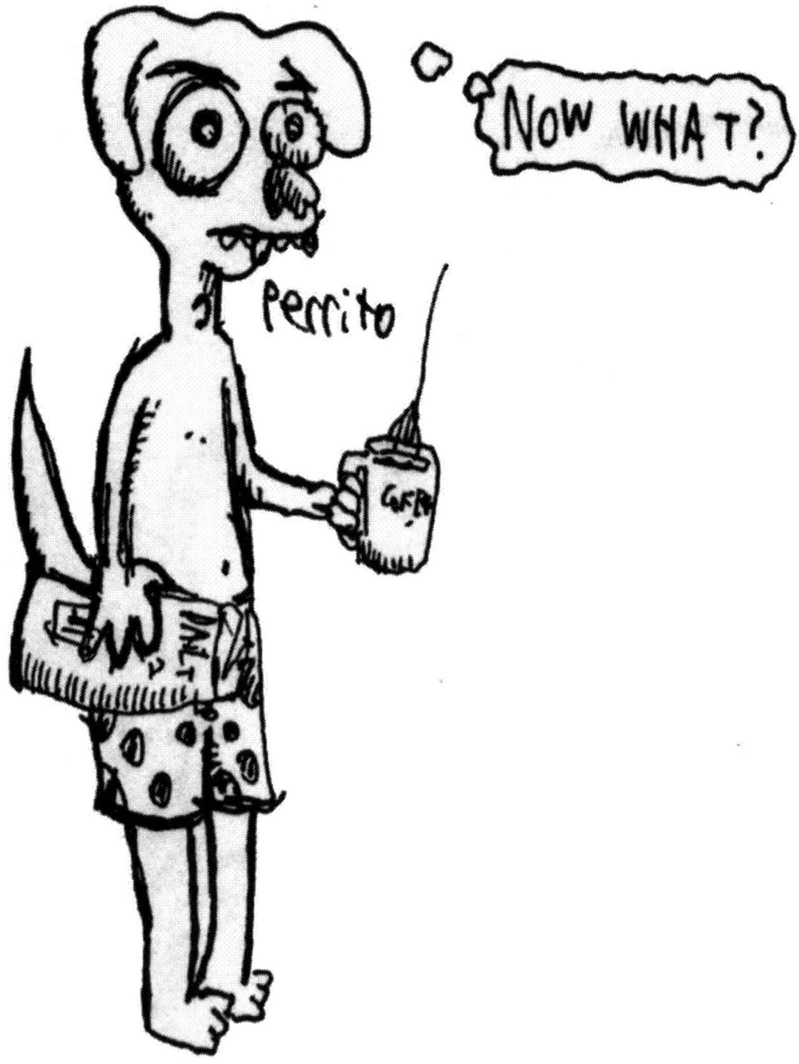
NOW WHAT?
perrito

`Gatorade`

Gatorade is a
non-carbonated sports drink
marketed by the Quaker Oats Company,
a division of PepsiCo.

Originally made
for athletes,
it is now commonly
consumed as a snack beverage.

The drink is intended
to rehydrate and
to replenish
the carbohydrates
(in the form of sugars sucrose and glucose)
and electrolytes (sodium and potassium salts)
depleted during aerobic exercise,
especially in warmer climates.

...

Wait! This is not a poem.
It's merely the beginning
of the Wikipedia article
about Gatorade!

`October, 2007`

Kerouac : His Muse :: Me : You

I love pen I love paper
I love this literary caper.
I love your face in iPhoto
as clear Ginsburg's glasses,
watching Jack Kerouac beat his muse
as she bleeds poetry.

71

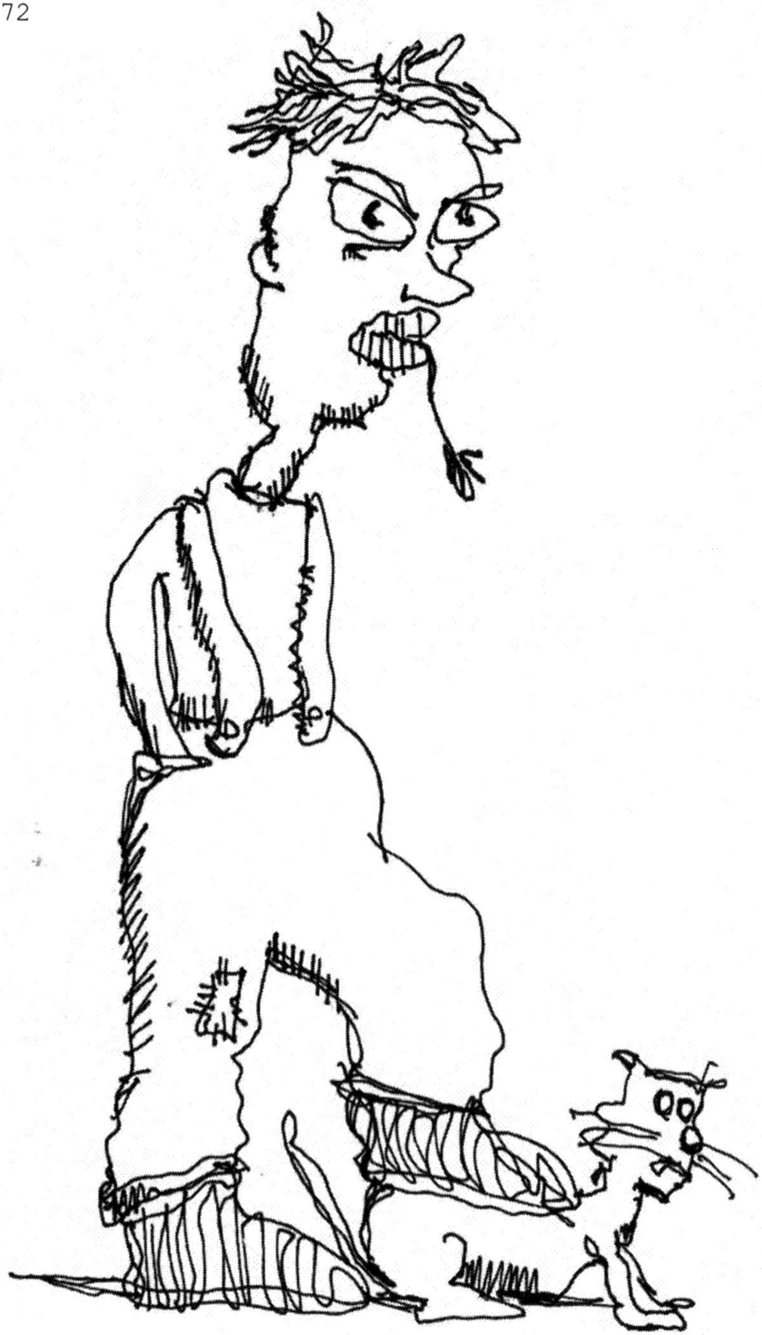

Bukwoski in Love

Some players were never meant to be house broken,
boning through time
meaningless interaction after meaningless interaction
skin on skin plus friction.

Tired of sex like Rivers Cuomo.

"But that's not sustainable"
Charles Bukowski once told me,
Drunk on whiskey in a Silver Lake bar
"I've spent my whole life with 1,000,000 lovers
and what do I have to show for it
besides my mountains of poems and stories
and trips to Planned Parenthood?"

"We're living life," I say,
"the players must play."

"I've lived my life," he said,
"angry at the world,
because my Helen of Troy tore my heart out.
So I stomped on hers
and any other chickadee
I could come across."

(pun intended)

`nerves`

nerves twitch in dark places
i can't describe -

nerves twitch as arteries and veins palpitate
in the lower part of my back -

nerves twitch as i tilt and attempt
to enter a room i know all too well is all too small.

      as thousands upon thousands join
      and yell and jerk and try to fit into similar holes,
      doing so on a scale of failure to four-point-oh!
          hoping to make that 4.3 and become oh so free!

nerves pull me back
and mentors edit _____ poems like this one.

nerves slowly wrap around my neck
and choke me as i fall to the floor:

      yet stubbornly i continue, trying to break out of
      this cocoon my neurotic parents have built for me...

"live a little" someone once said
as i writhed in the tightened umbilical cord:

          i cry for help and reach for the shears.

`April, 2000`

75

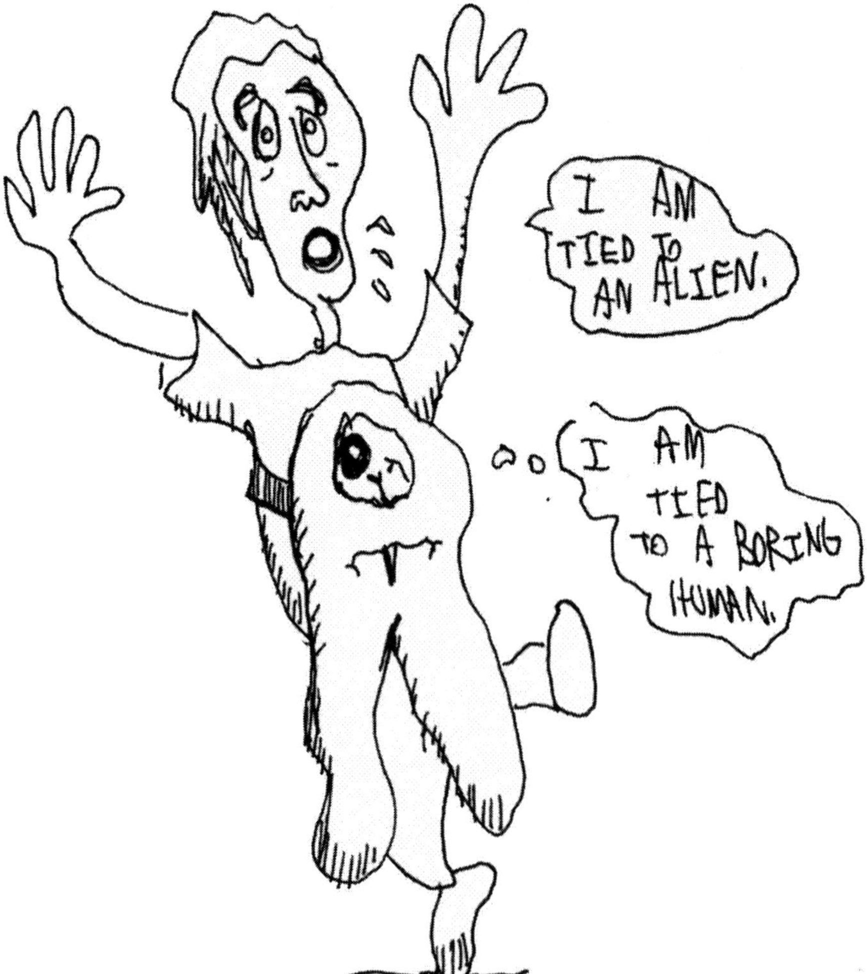
I AM TIED TO AN ALIEN.
I AM TIED TO A BORING HUMAN.

I Am an Alien

I am an Alien.
An alien!
Imagine
       that.

Hummm hummm so much
       fun
in my cute little craft that
       i
    lev   tates.

whirrr whirrr whirrrr go my cute little
motors   but watch the fuck out
      (because)

      my
cute little lasers aren't quite
      toys.

October, 1998

Confirmation Day

I genuflect at the altar of obscurity
One hand in the community wafers
The others between the Psalms
A leash tied to my esophagus

Forty-five Dalmatians in choirboy outfits
Jump up from underneath the pews
Barking in unison

They want something I can't decipher
Their eyes are as dead as a whale
Unspoken hunger

I feed Preparation H
To my hungry colon

The dogs circle
Growling angrily,
Sniffing at the sweet ointment

February, 2007

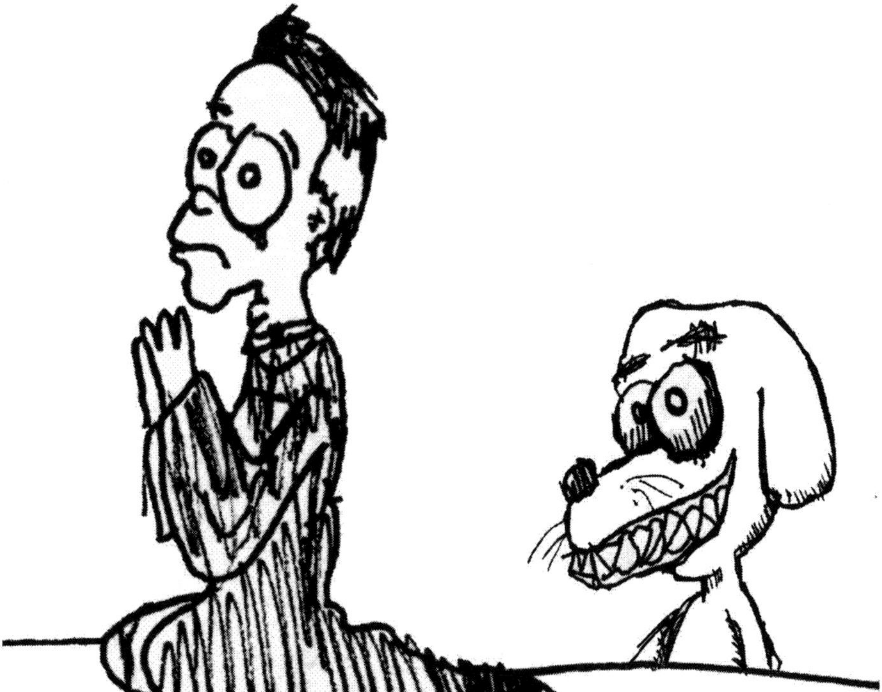

COME EXPLORE THE MYSTERIES OF THE DEEP, WITHOUT DIVING EQUIPMENT. UNLESS YOU WANT TO CLIMB OVER AND JUMP IN AND RISK GOING TO JAIL... JUST CLIMB INTO THE TANK.

The Hot Girl Who Works At This Summer Camp with Me Should Visit My Bunk More Often

This girl is so beautiful everyday
She is so happy, I'm inside
And I lied when I said I didn't want her here.
Look I swear I want to make it work
And rescue you again
I'm pulsating alone give a dog a loan
I want that physical rush horizontal,
Sweating obliquely.
Do you like that? I like you.
Here I can give you paradise.
Let's hang out, teach me about
Fallen Leaf Lake jellyfish, lateral moraines,
The geological history of Angora,
And I'll teach you how to paint it all.
You are too hot to be sleeping in your cabin alone
Let's make the shower gross together
After we rock the Hobart

Because that's what summer camp is for!

July, 2003

October 31, 1998

"What is that? Which planet?
Oh wait; that's a spaceship."
How adorable you are
When you stare up at the sky.

You run ahead of us,
With our masks and poorly done face paint.

We stand like criminals
And laugh occasionally,
And I remember the first day we met
So long ago…

But you eventually destroyed me with
Your casual indifference and
Heart-wrenching apathy.
Tonight you're the Yellow Flower
And I'm Gatsby from chapter five.

You spit on the sidewalk,
And it's embarrassing
How crudely cute you are.

I miss you, my moon baby.
Bring me back to your frigid planet
So you can break my heart
As we analyze the stars.

October, 1998

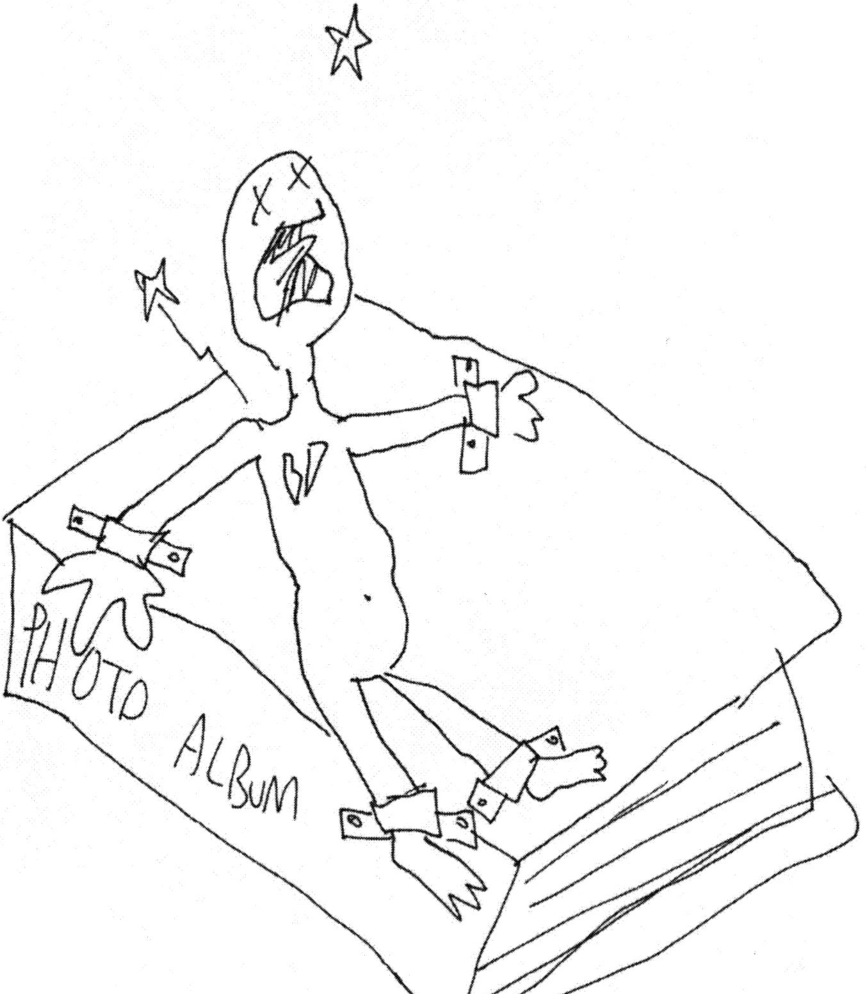
BD
PHOTO ALBUM

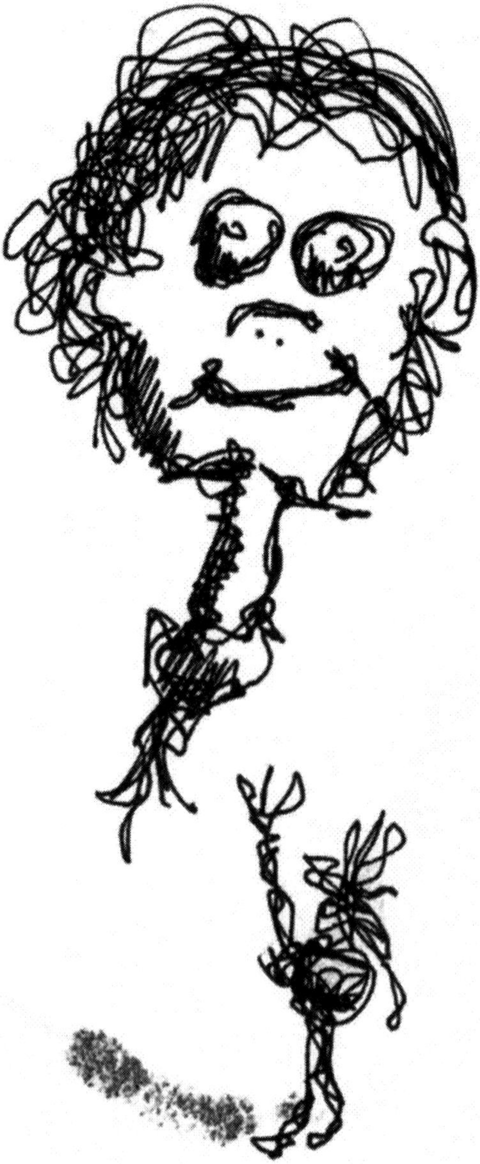

Stoned in Denver

I'm curled up in the corner
Your smiling face is on my screen again
And your big green eyes
And loving lips
Laugh at me
Loneliness is a cold laptop

All I wanted was serenity and calm
But Facebook beckoned again

I've had my fair shares of victories too
But it's so pyrrhic
When the space between now and then
Could fill 1,000 Grand Canyons

There's no messing around -
This Rocky Mountain High
Has certainly got me down tonight

Jealousy: the gift that keeps on giving

April, 2007

Shelf Life

And I kept my shelf neat-
Oh yes, as tidy as it could be,
Secretly situated in the crevice
I did my best to hide;
For only I had the right to see my dreams
As they collected dust throughout the years...

When it became time to decide
What I was to be,
I couldn't chose, because I didn't
Want to disorganize my shelf of dreams-
So I left it neatly situated in its place
Never having chosen any of the interesting roles
I had fondly imagined would
Suit me so well-

Now I am but one of the
Objects on a much larger shelf,
Kept in alphabetical order,
Not by size,
Since that would cause the boards to bend with unevenness.
I snugly sit between two others,
Surrounded by people
Who once boasted of
Having their shelves in order.

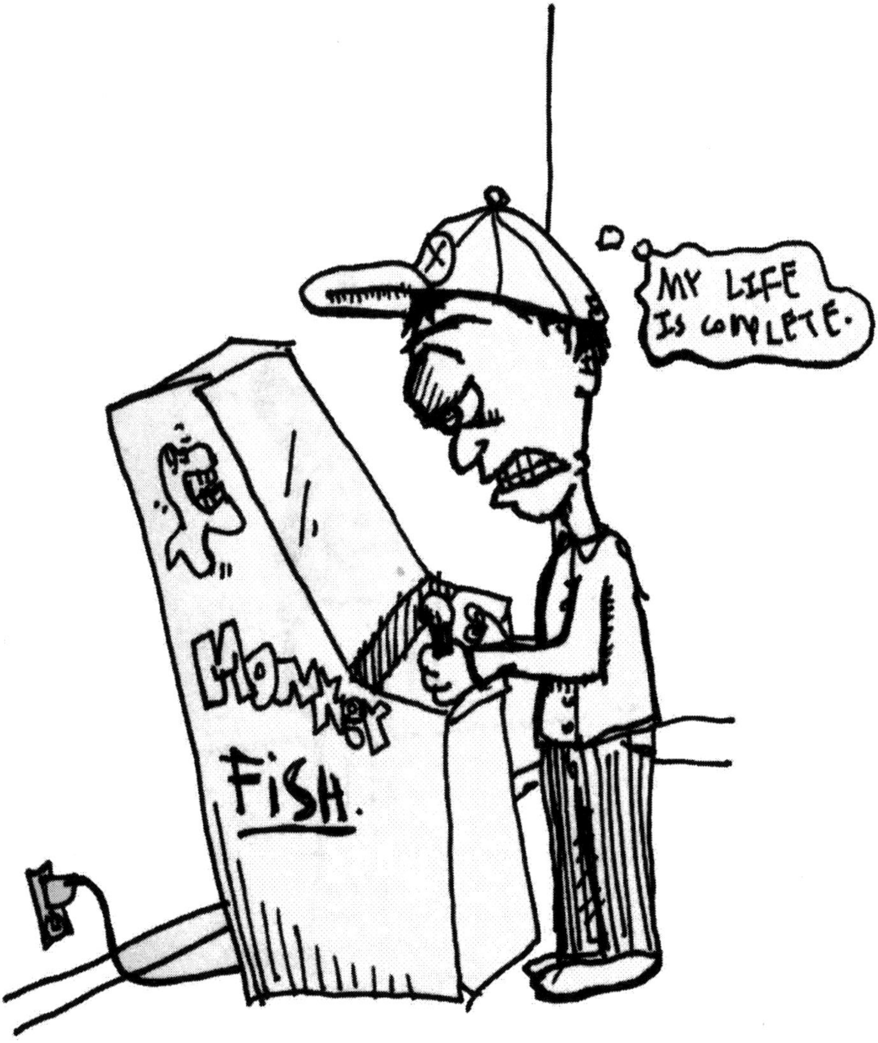
MY LIFE
IS COMPLETE.
FISH.

Kill the PAIN
create

http://www.mclars.com/data/bukowski.zip